STEVEN MICHAEL RAKES

WISDOM
from the HOLY
MOUNTAIN

LIFE LESSONS FROM
THE MONKS OF MT. ATHOS

I dedicate this book to my dear wife, Popie,
who has supported me throughout my life
and has encouraged me to write this book.
She is my best friend and helpmate.

TABLE OF CONTENTS

PROLOGUE

Over the past fourteen years, I have had the joy of traveling several times to Holy Mount Athos in northern Greece as a pilgrim. Mt Athos is a centuries old enclave of the Eastern Orthodox Church. There are 20 monasteries and various other skeets, huts and caves. The region is dedicated to the Mother of God and only men are allowed. The monks work, pray and worship together as a community. Pilgrims are allowed to visit and enter the life of the monastery. The Holy Mountain is for me a home away from home. I find peace and solace each time I visit. These trips have enriched my life and changed me as a person in Christ. I have traveled with friends as well as my two sons and my parish priest. Each of these visits was unique. When one travels to a place where prayer, worship, and spiritual struggle are the order of each day, a change occurs in the spirit and there is both growth and grace.

Traveling to the Holy Mountain is not a requirement or a necessity. One can come close to Christ and His Holy Church without ever spending time in monastic communities. I found that I was uplifted in a unique and special way by the fervor of the monks and the beauty of the worship. Many of the visits occurred during Pentecost. The worship during this season is particularly beautiful and moving.

While on the mountain, we stayed at the Iviron Monastery, and during these times we made visits to other monasteries and hermitages on the mountain. We were fortunate to spend many hours with the monks, and we had many discussions regarding spiritual life and human struggles. The monks met with us individually and as a group. We were allowed to ask questions and to inquire about the teachings of the Church. Our group was composed of fathers and sons from many walks of life. Dear friends were with me on these trips. The experience of traveling together to this holy place has made us all closer. Each monk spoke about matters that came up organically in group discussions. I made it my mission to take notes using notepads and my phone. It was a miracle to me that I was able to remember so much of what was said. I always believed that these notes would be for my friends, family, and me alone. It was not my intention to publish these gems. But during one of my visits, I shared some of this with a monk from Iviron and he said, "Do not hide what you have learned; share it with everyone." Although these thoughts were delivered by monks to men, I believe these teachings are not for men only but can enrich the lives of everyone who reads them.

What you will read in this collection is a summary of the notes I took on these visits, which spanned a fourteen-year period. Some of this is repetitive, and that reflects the number of times the monks emphasized a particular point. I want you, the reader, to be able to experience the information as I did. Just as we were able to ask the monks questions about different topics in our minds and hearts, the notes are presented here by topic in the hope that you might be able to read their wisdom about a topic close to your mind and heart, instead of feeling the need to read the story from beginning to end.

We were blessed to receive these words from holy men who, despite their spiritual struggle and daily duties, took the time to engage with us. These are the words and stories that were given to us, and I hope you can enjoy and learn from what is written, and that it may enrich your life as much as it has mine. I have left out the names of the monastic fathers to protect their privacy. Whenever possible, I will describe the monks without revealing their names.

One beautiful aspect of the monks I encountered was the positive encouragement that I received from them. Whenever I spoke negatively about myself or the way I was conducting my life, they always spoke words of encouragement, pointing out to me the good in my life and reminding me that life in the world is difficult and that my efforts toward spiritual growth were honored by God. This will be evident in some of the stories and passages that you read.

My hope is that this small book might be a companion for you to use as a source of encouragement and hope. May it be blessed!

HAPPINESS

The requirements for happiness are a clear conscience, gratitude or gratefulness, and hope in God, as well as patience and love.

Saint Isaac the Syrian says that sadness without hope from God is from the evil one.

Dorotheos of Gaza says that the humble man knows the truth and he knows himself. He says, "I made a mistake, but I will push forward in hope." Humility is in the middle. On one side is extreme (prideful) self-flagellation: "How could I do this? I can't believe that I could do this." On the other side is total denial and taking no responsibility for our actions. In the middle is the truth. Only God can heal our wounds.

—*Monk 1 from Iviron Monastery*

WISDOM

The soul is so deep that only God can know it.

Why should we chase the darkness? We should switch on the light and the darkness will leave on its own. We will allow Christ throughout our soul, and the demons will flee.

Someone can speak about their sins and be proud, and someone else can speak about their virtues and be humble.

Nobody can become a Christian by being lazy. It needs work—lots of work.

If you want, you can become holy even in the middle of a city.

God loves us very much. He has us in mind in each moment, and He protects us. We should know this and not be afraid of anything.

You should ask God to forgive you for your sins; and because you have asked Him humbly and with pain of heart, God will forgive you all your sins and it is His will to heal your body, too.

Great sorrow and sadness do not come from God; they are a trap set by the devil.

God takes care of the most intimate details of our life. He is not indifferent toward us. We are not alone in the world.

Fill your soul with Christ, with divine longing, with divine love, and with joy, and the joy of Christ will heal you.

Don't be concerned about others loving you, but with you loving Christ and others. This is the only way for the soul to be filled.

The most important thing of all is for people to love Christ, and all problems will be resolved.

It's not easy to be with a saint. He pushes you and sees your soul, but he gives light and hope.

The Holy Spirit comes to the reader from holy books.

The *Theotokos* (Birth giver of God) was with Christ on the cross. She never left him. When we enter the life of the Church (the cross, prayer, and fasting), she is with us, and we are united with her.

The Theotokos was a ladder, and the cross is also a ladder. Through Her birth giving the earth and heaven were united.

We enter His tomb with prayer and fasting (the desert), as did the Desert Fathers.

Saint Anthony was the first monastic. The demons attacked Anthony in the church, so he went into the desert, where he lived in solitude, was assaulted by demons, and was thought to be dead. "Lord where were you?" he cried.

God spoke to Saint Anthony and said, "I was watching your valor (as you fought the demons)!"

Once the church was legalized by Constantine in 312 AD, the fathers of the desert went to the wilderness to battle the demons. The desert is now inside of us.

Monasticism was an experiment at first by those seeking Him so they could serve Him at all costs.

Saint Athanasius was the champion of Orthodoxy and monasticism. He made it part of the life of the Church. The hallmark of a monastic is obedience to an elder or abbot.

—*Saint Porphyrios of Mount Athos*

He [Monk 2 from Xenophontos Monastery] spoke about the monastic effort. He said, "The monastic life is the lungs of the Church and breathes life into the whole Church and cleans the blood." This is an amazing medical observation for a simple monk without formal education.

On prayer, he referred to the Jesus Prayer and said this prayer is the key to knowledge of God.

The Orthodox Church is an ascetic church, and this ascetic practice is at the heart of everything.

Constant work is needed, especially in self-denial. In order to find true prayer, one must dedicate his life and make every action a prayer and movement to God. He said it is best to look back on life and assume everything so far was sinful. From this point forward, we have a new beginning.

He is a woodworker and was asked how he avoids pride in his beautiful works. He laughed and said, "who said I avoid pride? We all have it." He said that in this life we cannot create as was done in the days of old. He uses his talent to recreate the beauty of the past. He feels that technology has replaced culture. He referred to cement as an easy-to-work-with product that makes building easy, but it is not sustainable. The buildings on Mount Athos are more than 1,000 years old and were built—stone by stone—from local products that fit together naturally. This creates a healthy building that lasts for centuries. This is what created culture. Men lay and fit stone and wood to create beauty and art. This is no longer done in our society.

He said simplification of our lives and obedience makes prayer more possible. God's voice is hard to hear when there is anxiety and confusion. He cautioned against finding the easy way out, and encouraged us to make the most, not the least, effort in our life. This ascetical practice builds our strength as Christians, he said.

He said the Panagia will reward the effort we pilgrims made to come to the Holy Mountain.

The Theotokos is the Lady of the Mountain, and she is the depository of all the good in the Church and the highest among the saints. The eternal God received the gift of His earthly body from her. He encouraged us to share what we have learned. He said the gift of the Holy Mountain is hope in God and the love of the Theotokos. She is the Mother of us all, and she opens the way to God her Son.

—*Monk 2 from Xenophontos Monastery*

FAMILY LIFE

We hate to see our children suffer or make mistakes, but we must let them go. Our focus is to be an example to them. Don't preach, rather act, and let that take the place of spoken words. Trust God to guide them. Saint Porphyrios says, "Don't speak to your children about God, rather speak to God about your children."

—*Monk 1 from Iviron Monastery*

MARRIAGE

Young men who are searching for a job and a wife need to be strong in their faith. There are godly women, and God will send them to a man who lives a godly life. Be honest from the start with a woman. Know that life is a risk, and so is marriage a risk. With faith, love, and God's help, one can have a good life with their mate. Godly men must dedicate themselves to their relationship and decide: "I will marry this woman and be with her for sixty years" or "I will enter this monastery and stay for sixty years." Whether choosing to be a monk or to marry, there is never enough time to be sure, so committing is important, but only with the help of Christ.

The only difference between monastic life and married life is chastity. All of us are called to be monastics in our life. Monks are neither more spiritual nor more wise, only celibate. This is a difficult struggle.

—*Monk 1 from Iviron Monastery*

✝✝✝

Marriage success is on three levels: psychological, spiritual, and physical. All three must be in balance for a marriage to thrive. Be open, honest, and willing to discuss all things. Don't hold back.

By opening yourself to your spouse and speaking lovingly, the love between man and wife is purified and edified. Speaking harshly actually harms the other, and this is not what we want. Satan knows the weakness and attacks at that point, often subtly, allowing years to pass with no resolution. Don't allow this. Don't let things fester. This can lead to calamity.

—*Monk 3 from Iviron Monastery*

CHILDREN

They can go away from the path set forth by their parents. They make a life and are happy. We see this, but sometimes we are not happy. What do we do when this happens? Do we intervene? Do we force ourselves onto others and try to compel them? Saint Porphyrios says, "The parents should not talk constantly to their children about God, but to God about their children." Acquire peace. Do prostrations for your children, especially in the night, and for those who hate you or you have problems with.

Our disposition and prayers—good or bad—are felt by the person, no matter the distance.

You must be prayerful, and these hidden prayers to Christ will be felt by the person and will convert them. You cannot hide your feelings. The spirit of the person will feel and absorb the positive or negative emotions you carry. We must have trust in God and find our own inner peace. We are not in control; if we have hope and prayer, then we will find that, "His will be done."

Lead with love and prayer, not your words.

Be thankful for the crosses and pray for the salvation of all people.

Keep yourself and your feelings out of it. Pray for spiritual protection for the person who needs this, both your children and your enemies. This is a long process, and patience is needed to make this happen and for both you and them to see the light. We talk too much, but we don't listen.

Love for the other consists of letting them go into the hands and the grace of Christ. He knows all and weeps for us in our struggles that we face without Him.

Calm down, breathe, relax, and know that Christ knows all, and he will act. Focus on the love he has for you and for the ones you love.

Children must be free and placed into the hands of the Lord. The image of a fisherman applies. A large fish that fights needs to be reeled in slowly and carefully. If the fisherman pulls too hard, the line will snap, and the fish will be lost. Keeping the fish on the line and slowly pulling him toward the boat is key. It's good to allow the fish to swim freely, while never losing them to the line. This is how we address parenthood—slowly, progressively pulling and guiding the catch to the boat.

It is good to have rules and to be strict, but only in a loving and respectful way.

Do not over-praise children. They get used to this and it puffs them up. It's a hard balance. We must encourage children without causing them to be prideful or arrogant.

Nurture children to virtue. Use compliments that emphasize virtue, like, "I saw that you worked hard and had great patience." You must let them know that virtue is key.

Be light. Praise the effort, not the outcome.

Humor is important. Smile, laugh, and trust.

—*Unnamed Monks*

OBEDIENCE

Obedience is freedom. For a monastic, giving up his will to a loving and wise abbot is true freedom and brings peace. Marriage and family bring peace to the couple, because they know their duties and their program, and no longer need to wonder and stress about what life will bring. Marriage is difficult, but at least a pious couple will know their roles in the relationship.

Don't try to force your friends and neighbors to speak to you and to acknowledge you. Give them room and respect. Be obedient, even to your children. Don't become angry. Obedience to children means showing them respect and love while being firm and guiding them.

Do not complain. It will make you weak and tired. Do whatever job is in front of you without complaining, and it will be easier.

—Monk 1 from Iviron Monastery

ON BALANCE

The abbot always refers to acquiring simplicity, purity, true humility of heart, and gentleness, along with balance, as the answers for everything. He was asked about many things but came back to these things as the means of attaining grace in life.

Focus on balance and order. Balance means the correct amount of work, rest, and recreation. Work is good, but there is a need to come home and detach from work to spend time with family in discussion. Entertainment is good, but do not have too much to eat and drink. This balance and order, along with what is mentioned above, lead to inner peace, which radiates to others.

Be sure to place order into your life. Regulate things with food, work, rest, exercise, and so on. This will make it easier to come closer to God.

This kind monk said it is good to come to Mount Athos to see that the traditions have been preserved and are lived.

The monks are steadfast, and they remain. We, too, must be steadfast and strive to remain in the fight.

At the monastery there is true equality, and everyone can speak and be heard. There are no rich and no poor. All tasks are shared, and this monastic life is a model for all life. Laypersons must incorporate these monastic traits into their lives so that, through daily prayer, fasting, ascesis, love, peace, and true humility, their home will become like a small Mount Athos. This is how we take the Holy Mountain home with us.

The Orthodox Church is different in its approach to life (than the Protestant faith). It preserves and embraces the ancient traditions but addresses the present-day needs of mankind. Perhaps Protestants are more focused on today's issues, and Judaism more on tradition. Orthodoxy focuses on both. Orthodoxy works to help people become better and lifts them up. The capitalist system creates an environment where individuals are pushed to conform and become part of the system, cogs in the wheel. In the capitalist system, all things are done to become a better worker, to make a living. People in the world are seen in relation to their value to the process or business, rather than their value to God. People in the West go to school, not to enrich their minds but to learn a vocation.

In all things, humility and love are the key. This does not mean we sit idle and do not speak. With love, we must speak against wrong. We must not judge people, but we can and should look at various systems, such as Islam, Mormonism, and so on, and judge them against the Orthodox tradition. While we have the truth, we must be humble and live our Orthodoxy fully. This is the best sermon we can give to others.

Speaking about the truth is less effective than living the truth.

There are three levels of passions according to Saint Isaac: love of money, love of power, and love of glory. The Church can help with this.

TV preachers say things they know are not true. This emanates from insecurity about their own ministry, unlike Orthodoxy, which understands its roots and addresses the heart of man in today's world.

This beautiful monk is filled with the peace, love, and humility that he spoke about. His words were always spoken gently and in love. Even when we spoke about evil or bad events in the world, he would say, "There is good and bad in all people."

—*Monk 3 from Iviron Monastery*

WORLDLY LIFE

According to Saint John Chrysostom, the meaning of life consists of three things. First, we come from God and are loved by Him. Second, we must become holy. To become holy, the Church is the vehicle and acquiring the virtues (love, joy, peace, humility, etc.) is the method. Third, we will return to God in the end.

Life is like the flight of a bird to a destination. We try to travel in a straight line to Christ, but the environment causes us to veer off the path, like a bird that faces bad weather, hunters, or predators. Still, the destination is the same: the Kingdom of God.

For decisions in life, we need a strong base: prayer, church services, fasting, and sacraments. If we lead a spiritual life, our decisions will be strong, and we need not worry. God's love will be sufficient. Never forget that God is like the athletic coach who puts us through workouts, not to harm us but to form us and prepare us for the future.

God sends trials for good (ascesis). The word ἄσκησις is a Greek word that has an athletic connotation. It means struggle or work done to develop strength and endurance. In monastic terms, it refers to prayer, fasting, and spiritual struggles to come closer to Christ.

Love and a non-judgmental attitude are paramount. If someone says, "You are stupid!" then instead of anger and offense ask yourself, *Am I stupid?* or think, *perhaps my brother is struggling and that's why he says these harsh things to me.* Calm down and later ask him, "My brother, earlier you said I am stupid. Are you alright, and have I offended you?" Love and humility are the key. Instead of taking offense, we should humble ourselves when we face criticism. In all circumstances, we should examine and accuse ourselves before we judge others. When we see wrongdoing or sin, we must examine ourselves and ask if we could have helped the situation or prevented this from occurring. Saint John Chrysostom says, "Place yourself beneath all people, and you will find yourself in the presence of Christ."

This monk offered the following story as an illustration. Two monks were on their way to Church and decided to stop at the cell of one of their brothers to ask him to accompany them. When they knocked on his door, the door swung open and what they saw was shocking. The room was so disorderly they could not believe it. The first monk said, "I am scandalized by what I see. How can a monk live like this?"

The other monk replied, "Each evening in the middle of the night, I can hear this brother doing prostrations, chanting hymns, and saying prayers. If I prayed as he does, my room would also be disorderly. I have neither the strength nor the faith to pray as he does." We should never judge people because the truth is often a hidden reality that only

God knows. The monks each saw the same thing, but what they concluded was quite different. Sometimes we can see the sin and error of our brethren, but what we cannot see is the suffering and repentance. Always look for the good in people.

Monastic life can, at times, be a heavy load. Each day is not paradise. We must stay the course. It is important to remember that improving yourself is not for you alone, but also lifts those around you. This is true of both spiritual matters and personal matters such as one's career. Saint Seraphim states that if you save yourself and acquire a spirit of peace, thousands will be saved with you.

—*Monk 1 from Iviron Monastery*

Don't worry about work and money, rather worry about your soul. Sorrow that is shared is halved. Joy that is shared is doubled. Bitter medicine is needed for sweet health. According to Saint Isaac the Syrian, temptations lead to spiritual strength.

—*Monk from Vatopedi Monastery*

WORK

I [Steven] was discussing my life with one of the monks at Iviron. We were in the *trapeza* (dining area) of the monastery. I was lamenting that my life seemed consumed with work and essentially nothing else. He replied, "So, Stavros [my name in Greek], you work all the time, correct?" He asked me to follow him to the courtyard outside of the trapeza. There is a large bird's nest there where the local birds feed and fly in and out. The monk said, "You see, Stavros, the birds work both day and night and never stop. They work to feed their children and to provide a strong nest for their family." He then said, "Now listen. Do you hear how the birds sing with joy as they work? This is what you must do. As you are working, do not fret or be sorrowful, but rather sing Psalms and hymns with joy. Work is good, and God will bless your work if you do it with joy and in praise of Him. Make the work that you do a prayer and give thanks always, with joy and gratitude to Christ who gives you this opportunity." Amen.

—*Monk 1 from Iviron Monastery*

PRAYER

Pilgrims do not have the time to pray like monks. We can, however, make our life into prayer. If we look at all we do from the eyes of the Church and Christ, then all things become prayer. Our job or work, if focused on the care and love of our family and others, becomes a prayer.

—Monk 1 from Iviron Monastery

Prayer comes naturally when cultivated in the soil of obedience and humility. This leads to inner peace. Pray for God's peace and His will. Prayer can bubble to the surface.

The Bible does not prescribe anything (such as praying for health) except to submit to the will of God, and all the things like health and peace will be fruits of this effort. The good things we pray for, like health, stability, happiness, and so on, are given to us if we attain a peaceful and humble heart.

—Monk from Vatopedi Monastery

ACHIEVEMENT

Competition in work is not good. Other forms of competition are good if you do your best—for example, sports competitions. Money and success are all vanity and will not lead to peace and joy. People find that after a lot of success, they are empty. The need to be first is the ego.

We need to be grateful in all things, and not look at the results of our actions.

—Monk 1 from Iviron Monastery

PASSIONS

Passions are like wild dogs that chase after us. When we see wild animals, we run away. We do not play with the passions. They are fierce and hungry, and they hunt for us. We run from them to Christ. If we engage the passions, they will destroy us just like wild dogs.

—*Monk 1 from Iviron Monastery*

CHARITY

C harity is more than giving money to poor people. It also involves forgiving and loving people who have hurt or offended you.

—*Monk 1 from Iviron Monastery*

WATCHFULNESS (ΝΕΙΠΣΙΣ)

Watchfulness is the way to battle thoughts. Nous is the eye of the soul or heart. It relates more to the inward spirit of a person. These are the subconscious parts of a person. This is where we experience God and sense His presence.

Soul = nous, where we've experienced God.

You can contain the whole world in your heart, and you can pray for all people. This is holiness.

We are continually attacked by Satan. The closer we come to Christ, the more intense are the attacks. Expect temptation, as it is a sign of progress. As you get closer to God, the temptations become more intense.

Stay active in the body to avoid these thoughts.

Gifts are given to us, not to make us happy but to share with others and to share with the world. If it's about us, then we're never happy or joyful.

Saint Sophrony says that if you love yourself, you will hate God.

We have an enemy: Intrusive thoughts can take us away from prayer.

Saint Athanasias said, "Temptation consists of evil thoughts. To avoid them, use the name of Jesus Christ." Saint Silouan calls them internal voices.

Saint John Cassian said, "It is impossible not to be troubled. We expel evil thoughts with prayer."

Don't despair. This is the goal of the evil one. Our Lord allows us to be tempted to our strength.

Self-exploration is an important function. What is really bothering you?

Where is God? What happens when holy people don't pay attention to me as a person? We are sensitive.

Saint Sophrony says everything in the world today fights against our prayer. The arena is the heart. We have a guardian angel. The Jesus Prayer can cause the demons to attack, but they are afraid of the guardian angel. When you wander in prayer, you must call to Christ and your guardian angel.

Throw the invocation of the name of Christ into the intrusive thoughts, and they will disperse.

We must pray for the person who bothers us. The person who bothers us is (in spiritual terms) our enemy. We must pray for our enemies if we want to attain eternal life.

Saint Isaac the Syrian says, "Consider every prayer which you utter in the night to be of greater worth than all of the activities of the day."

—*Unnamed Monks*

SAINT PORPHYRIOS

This story was told to us about Saint Porphyrios.

Elder Porphyrios was meeting with an abbess at a monastery in Athens and said he had to leave. He took two nuns with him and got in a taxi. He told the nuns not to say a word. The driver was rude and very critical of the Church. He taunted the nuns and said the monks are crooks and homosexuals.

The Elder told the driver, "I have a story for you." He told the story of a murder on the outskirts of Athens. A woman was raped, killed, and thrown into the sea. The Elder slapped his hands on his knees and repeatedly said, "But we can't find the murderer!"

The taxi driver stopped the car and asked Elder Porphyrios to come out of the cab and confessed, "I am the murderer, and you are a prophet." This was witnessed by the two nuns who were in the taxi with him who the elder told not to speak, no matter what they heard in the cab, until his death. The Abbess still tells the story today. The taxi driver repented, and the Elder was his spiritual father. The Abbess told the story to Abbott Vasilios of Iviron, who told the monks the story. The monks of Iviron say Elder Porphyrios, now Saint Porphyrios, had more charisma than any other modern saint.

—*Monk 1 from Iviron Monastery*

DEMONS

W e fight against demons, and we can succeed. They have no power unless we allow it. Christ cast the demons into the pigs, and immediately the pigs cast themselves into the sea. The man had the demons in him for many years, and those demons could not destroy him. Despite his possession, the possessed man had the Holy Spirit buried deep inside him. The demons had power over animals, but not man. So, resist and do not be afraid. You are the one who grants power to evil.

—*Monk 1 from Iviron Monastery*

TEMPTATION

Temptation is a gift. Saint Isaac says we cannot progress in our Christian walk without temptation. Just like in athletics, we perform difficult exercises to trim the fat. We need temptation because we are all spiritually fat.

—*Monk 1 from Iviron Monastery*

ON *LOGISMOI*

*L*ogismoi are intrusive thoughts from demons or from within that take us away from God. Avoid them and know they are planted by the evil one (Satan).

Patience and obedience are cardinal virtues.

—*Unnamed Monks*

THOUGHTS

Don't always believe your thoughts. They can mislead. Speak to someone, such as your spiritual father or a friend, to flush out the issue before your thoughts take over. Make everything a prayer. Remember that love can conquer your fear and your bad thoughts. Go inside yourself to see your faults and shortcomings but reach out to others because their pain is often the result of feeling unloved.

We do not fight evil thoughts. Saint Isaac the Syrian says to resist evil thoughts with prayer. The monastics practice the "prayer of the heart" (Jesus Prayer), *Καρδιακή Προσευχή*. The prayer is "Lord Jesus Christ, Son of God, have mercy on me, a sinner." In a shorter form, one can say, "Lord, have mercy on me, a sinner." This form of prayer reflects the teaching of Saint Paul to "pray without ceasing." The prayer is repeated to keep the mind focused on Christ. The constant recitation can lead to the prayer bubbling up and continuing in the heart, even during sleep. The monks suggested finding a spiritual guide to help learn and practice this hesychastic, ancient form of prayer. The saints throughout time have used this prayer and have taught it to their followers. The monks recite this softly throughout the course of their day.

The prayer rope (*Koboskini*) is held in the hand and used to remind the person to pray the prayers consecutively. The prayer rope is referred to as the sword used to enter the arena of battle against sin and passions. We witnessed these monks in prayer all the time. Patience was emphasized in the use of the Jesus Prayer. Pilgrims are anxious to succeed at prayer but acquiring prayer of the heart is a process that takes years of practice. We witnessed the absolute joy that these very devout and holy monks had because they had perfected the inner prayer of the heart. Despite this hard road to pure prayer, we were encouraged to say the prayer whenever possible. One monk compared the Jesus Prayer to a home at night. Thieves can approach the house to rob and steal. If they come to the door of the house and hear voices inside, the robbers flee knowing that the house is occupied. The Jesus Prayer, when recited continually, is like this. Satan comes to the door of your heart, but when he hears the Jesus Prayer ("Lord, have mercy on me, a sinner") he flees, knowing the heart is occupied by the prayer. This was a beautiful and encouraging image.

Patience and gratefulness are the key to moving through dark times. We must not be anxious but wait and know that God is working His will for us. Be patient. We want gratification instantly. Always say, "Thy will, Lord, not mine." With this attitude, His plan will be revealed, and we can then accept it with joy.

Don't fight bad thoughts but go immediately to prayer. Even if you win a battle with Satan, he has thousands of years of experience battling Christians. The smell of the battle will linger on you. Let God fight the fight.

We often become tired because we let our thoughts rule us. We complain, and this makes us tired.

We have been hurt and wounded in the past, and we should expect to be hurt again. We must draw a red line and say, "Enough! Now I must go forward with the help of God." As Elder Porphyrios says, "Every attack of the demons is an opportunity to turn to God." Use these attacks to move toward Christ. This is very difficult, but we face each moment as it comes, and we do not listen to the evil thoughts.

—*Monk 1 from Iviron Monastery*

ASCESIS

Is it chosen or given to us? Life has what you need. Some people deprive themselves of comfort and luxury. This monk told us that the "world" does not understand true sacrifice or ascesis. Monastic life is a good model.

Blindness and deafness are a spiritual exercise. They are both a true form of deprivation. Ascetical struggles are chosen, but blindness and deafness must be endured without a person's choice. Blind or deaf people are closed to the world. There were pilgrims at the monastery who were deaf. We pilgrims who speak English complain about all the Greek language used at the monastery, but these men can't hear anything, Greek or English.

—*Monk 3 from Iviron Monastery*

Family life itself is a form of ascesis. Love of others is a crucifixion. Just as Christ spread out his hands on the cross, we open our arms to others and sometimes we suffer. We sacrifice for our children and spouses, and many parents walk away from this responsibility. This life—family—is ascesis and struggle, with family and work responsibilities, and so on. The prayers of a layman —a family man—are perhaps, in God's eyes, higher than monastic prayer, due to the burdens of family life. This monk said that prayer in the monastery is easy due to the quiet, orderly life of the monastics. He said that in the world, men have many responsibilities and burdens. If a man in the world can pray from his heart for even five minutes, God will honor that prayer even more than the eight to nine hours of prayer from the monk. This was great encouragement to all of us.

For monastics, hospitality is a new form of ascesis. It is difficult, but the monks are encouraged by pilgrims who are seeking God in a difficult and unloving world. Amidst the noise and activity, even the intention to pray is honored by God. A consistent, small amount of prayer may, in many ways, be more precious to God than the long prayers of the monastics.

It is important not to confuse regret with repentance. Regret is self-centered: "How could I sin over and over?" This is ego, and not of God. Repentance is realizing that, "I am a sinner, and I will sin again." The key is not how many times I fall, but rather, with God's grace, how many times I rise. I must go beyond being humiliated and be willing to be humbled.

Saint John Cassian said if one man is naturally calm and humble, and another man is naturally easy to anger but struggles and only improves slightly, God may honor the latter more than the first for his effort. Struggle against passions is honored by God.

This monk told the following story: A man in the Church of Xenophontos was crying during church, and a wise and humble monk asked him to venerate the icon of Panagia. As he leaned in to venerate and kiss the icon, the monk said, "Stop. What do you see?" The man said, "It is dark and blurred." The monk replied, "Now, kiss the icon and stand back." After the man venerated, the monk asked as he stood back, "Now what do you see?" He said, "I see Panagia." The point was that we often do not see holiness during the storm. Like the Apostles, we sometimes can't see Christ in the storm because we don't have the eyes to see. It is important to see the beauty inside stormy times, which are sent to us by God for edification and growth.

We must be peaceful and pray, but even the Apostles struggled with this. When they saw Christ walking on the water in the storm, even though they knew him intimately, they still thought they saw a ghost. Never forget that the Apostles were men who struggled with their belief, as we do today.

Mary of Egypt was cast out of the Church due to her sinfulness. She is an icon of repentance and healing of the image of God in us. She did not ignore the image of Christ inside her. She restored the icon and therefore returned her image to pure humanity through repentance. She became one with nature, and even the wild animals recognized her pure humanity. We must look at difficult people and difficult situations as tarnished icons that need restoration. We venerate these people as holy images, and we pray for their restoration.

He described family and monastic life as sharp rocks rubbing against each other and slowly, over time, becoming smoother. This is life. We rub against one another, and this softens and smoothes us.

He told the story of a miracle-working icon that was taken from the Holy Mountain several years ago for veneration in a church in Thessaloniki. He said people lined up and venerated from 7 a.m. to 1 a.m. It was hard to stop the people from coming. He saw this as a good sign for people in Greece seeking sanctity.

—*Monk 3 from Xenophontos Monastery*

SPIRITUAL LIFE

Balance is important in the spiritual life. We cannot trust in God suddenly, but rather we must slowly give ourselves to Him. Be patient. Spiritual life and struggle require patience. If we try to be excessive in the spiritual life, we will harm both ourselves and our path to Christ, just like excessive physical training can harm the body.

The Church is a gift and makes our life more tolerable. Since we are in the Church, we can cope with life's problems. We must be immersed in the life of the Church, and this will help us develop our conscience, which will guide us. Mistakes are common, and we must not worry about that possibility. Just let God take over.

—*Monk 1 from Iviron Monastery*

The image of Orthodoxy is Christ on a boat in a storm. The storm rages around us, but we stay inside the boat, the Church. We should live each week as if it were Holy Week. Every day of the week carries meaning as it did at the time of Christ's passion.

Do what needs to be done, and don't try too hard to understand what is good and evil. Your life is your prayer. Be honest and ethical and do all things in love and with prayer. Don't think, but rather be active in doing good.

—*Monk 2 from Iviron Monastery*

ORTHODOXY

O rthodoxy is a religion characterized by sobriety and dispassion. We have a less-emotional approach, and we live our spiritual life in a patient and serious manner. We don't ignore our emotions, but they cannot define us.

—*Monk 4 from Iviron Monastery*

HOLY RELICS

O ne evening during our discussions, one of the young men from our group brought up the issue of holy relics and wondered why the Church venerates them. We were told that the grace of the Holy Spirit descends upon saintly and holy people. When this happens, that grace comes upon both the spirit and the physical body of the holy one. At the time of death, that grace remains on the body. That is why the bodies of holy saints can remain uncorrupted after their death. The monk said that this mirrors the Garden of Eden, where paradise was characterized by perfect and uncorrupted existence.

We were taken to the reliquary, where the relics of many holy saints were kept for veneration. The monk explained to us that he had lived there for twenty years and had visited this reliquary to pray and meditate many times. Despite the heat and moisture, he had never seen any spoilage or corruption of the human tissue in the room. He asked those of us in the medical field if we had ever witnessed human flesh essentially preserve itself. He said to me, "Dear doctor, how would you explain this phenomenon?" In the room were the hands, feet, fingers, limbs, and appendages of holy men and women from hundreds of years ago. These items were intact and had not lost their integrity. We were all astounded by the reality that confronted us at that moment.

After this, we went into the ossuary where the skeletal remains of deceased monks are kept. Father described this as his future home. He asked, "Do you see rich men, poor men, wise men, or saints?" We must all realize that this life is temporal, and we must strive for the kingdom, which is not of this world.

—*Monk 1 from Iviron Monastery*

CONFESSION

You must have confession as often as possible and do not lose contact with your spiritual father. In other words, don't wait too long between confessions. The spiritual father's knowledge of you and who you are is the way he is able to help you. If you often touch base and discuss things with your spiritual father, it will allow him to know you. Having a close spiritual father who knows your heart is a key element of the spiritual life. This is especially true for young people who struggle in this lonely world. Confession should not only be a listing of sins but a conversation about those things that weigh us down and bother us. There are no stupid questions or comments. Addressing trouble when it is small is like a doctor finding a tumor early, so it can be removed without harm to the one who is sick. When you confess, it brings earthly and heavenly humility. This is because your deeds are no longer hidden. You must see the priest, and he knows you and your heart.

—*Monk 1 from Iviron Monastery*

SYRIAN DESERT FATHERS AND SYRIAC IMAGERY

Saint Ephrem, the great poet, and Saint Romanos the Melodist were cut off from Byzantium.

The Syriac fathers are believed to have written the Odes of Solomon. They expressed theology in poetry, which is a hallmark of Syrian theology.

Markion was a heretic of Syria. Most Syriacs were comfortable with the Jewish origin and imagery of the Old Testament. To learn more, read Saint Ephrem's *Hymns on Paradise*.

Saint Romanos was a student of Saint Ephrem. They wrote theology in poetry based on the Old Testament.

✝✝✝

Bridal chamber, clothed in divinity, ladder, and so on are all Syriac imagery, including *heart, luminous eye,* and *tomb of the heart.* The demons don't want to be around Christ. He chases them out of the tomb of the heart.

Saint Dionysius of Syria wrote about hierarchy. We don't like it in the modern world. It is the ladder, the cross, or the Theotokos. The roots of the hierarchy of the Church are the Theotokos and the cross, the humility and love for mother and son, and vice versa. This is the essence of the faith. Without the Theotokos, the Church is an oppressive dogmatism. She is a cascade of light and love. All of this is Syrian. The heart becomes a font of love and thanksgiving for one who has come out of himself through this hierarchy.

God is impelled to come out of himself because of his erotic love of man. God moves toward us.

The Church is the bridegroom of Christ. His love for His Church is the basis of the love in a marriage. The couple long to be with each other and to commune in a fashion that is like the eros that God has for the Church. Marriage is holy because it mirrors the passionate love that God has for His Church and His people.

—*Syrian Desert Fathers*

COMMUNION

What is the most important state to be in when having communion? A state of good will and forgiveness. This is more important than even confessing mistakes. If you don't have a heart willing to forgive your enemies, then you shouldn't partake of the Eucharist.

—Monk 1 from Iviron Monastery

FASTING

What should I eat? As much as needed, says Abbott Vasileos. Don't tell others what to do. Don't waste but save the food. When someone gives you food, eat what you want. If you take it, eat it.

—*Monk 1 from Iviron Monastery*

EVANGELIZATION

Don't be concerned about converting others to Orthodoxy. Work on yourself, and this solid psychological–spiritual base will transform others and you will become a light. Non-Orthodox people have their religion, too, and God will save them where they are. When we speak to others about spiritual matters, we should be gentle and not scandalize them. Don't make people feel bad by pretending you are better or by being harsh or mean.

Speak with your heart and not your head.

The monks would often say to us that "God is everywhere" (*Ο θεός εναι παντού*). This means that the truth is not confined to the Orthodox Church. God reveals himself in His unique way to all people. This is reflected in the following quote from Saint Seraphim: "Acquire a spirit of peace and thousands will be saved with you." Focusing on our own spiritual growth is the best form of evangelizing or converting people to Christ and His Church. Trying to convert others when you are not yet purified can be a recipe for spiritual pride. Metropolitan Anthony Bloom says, "People will forgive the sinner you are, but not the saint you pretend to be."

—*Monk 1 from Iviron Monastery*

Don't judge people. God is the perfect union between justice and mercy. The word of Christ will judge them. Our job is to love them and realize that God loves them as much as He loves us.

Saint Paul did not preach to the masses but spoke to audiences receptive to his words. Evangelism is a special call, one that requires knowledge and strength. He went first to the Jews, and then moved on to others as he saw their readiness to hear. He was an apostle, and even he did his evangelizing carefully and with a sober and prayerful attitude. Some will be called to preach, but not everyone. We don't want to soft-pedal judgment, even though we ourselves are told, "Don't judge." To be a teacher or evangelist requires purification, enlightenment, and, ultimately, *theosis* (deification). So, the notion that we are to convert others is not scriptural. We need to become holy before we try to convince others. The world has not yet heard the gospel of the Orthodox Church, but only the western gospel. So, the end times have not come.

Speak with Protestants about the Mother of God. This shows the love the Orthodox Church has for women. The Church honors women because God Himself chose a woman to be the vehicle of His incarnation. The Church Fathers state that God looked down on all human history and found only one who was worthy to give birth to Him. God waited for the Theotokos before He entered His creation.

Her beautiful purity was noticed by the creator of the universe. The eternal God carries the humanity he received from the Theotokos into the Trinity. She is first among the Saints of the Church. She is the "ladder" that unites heaven and earth. We must never cease to ask for her prayer and intercession.

Only God knows who will be saved. He judges each according to their circumstances. Even though it says there is no salvation outside of Christ, He will reveal himself to each person in his unique and supernatural way. Many evangelicals are coming to the knowledge that they lack liturgical life and are turning to Orthodoxy.

—*Monk 4 from Iviron Monastery*

FAITH

One pilgrim came to the monastery at Xenophontos and said he had been away from the Church for forty years (since the age of fifteen). He felt something special, and wanted to meet with Geronda Alexios, the abbot. He was moved and had a confession with Geronda. Abbot Alexios said, "Tomorrow, I will give you communion." The pilgrim replied, "I cannot take the body and blood of Christ because I am a sinner." Abbot Alexios replied, "Because you have said you are a sinner, I will commune you. If you had said otherwise, then you would be truly unworthy."

Simplicity of heart is the key to the knowledge of God. The mind and logic separate us from God. Everyone has a different logic, but our hearts can be united. The abbot looked around the room and smiled, "You all are thinking something different." We must seek God with our heart and not our logic.

Anxiety is lack of faith. God does not allow temptation beyond what we are able to withstand. Living in the world requires prayer. The blessed life consists of praying for yourself and for others. This is the example of the monastery and the monks. They live with each other and support each other in the light of the worship and love of the Church. Consider that your anxiety is a call to fight for God's mercy. He will hear us, and He will help. He gives us what we need, not what we want.

The Liturgy sanctifies us, even if we don't commune. Attend the liturgy because it can heal.

Children should not be lectured to, but rather loved and given a holy example. The abbot told a story of a mother who prayed for a wayward son. Her son was the only one of her three children who had rejected the Church. This mother prayed on her knees in front of the icon of the Theotokos every night for her son to be reunited with the Church. When her son came home drunk one evening, he saw his mother in front of the icon and said, "Mom, I know you are there on your knees for me." He not only repented, but also became a monk! The abbot said, "How can God ignore such faith (of the mother)?!!"

—*Monk (Alexios) of Xenophontos Monastery*

The abbot [Alexios] told the story of a priest who was told to abort a child because they were told that the child and the mother (the priest's wife) were at risk. He sought the guidance of Saint George and Geronda (Alexios). "Geronda, what should I do?" Before he gave advice, Geronda said, "We must pray all night." God revealed to him (Alexios) that the child would be born normal, and the mother would be fine. He said, "Name the child George." The priest said that the doctor said it would be a girl. Geronda said, "Then name her Georgia." The child was born, and everything turned out as the holy man stated. It turned out the doctors were also wrong about the gender, and the child was a boy. The priest had recently come to the monastery to give the joyous news to Alexios.

Another man was devastated by the loss of his voice. All the doctors said it was a very difficult and unusual case. The man was told by the abbot to pray to Saint George, and subsequently he had a dream.

In the dream, he saw Saint George riding on a white horse. Saint George said, "Jump on the horse, and I will teach you to sing." In the morning he woke and was healed with a normal voice. "Faith does save," according to the abbot.

Coldness of the heart slowly warms if you stay focused on prayer.

God loves all people and judges them according to their knowledge. He is φιλάνθρωπος (lover of man). Protestants are not in danger because their hearts are good, but they lack knowledge.

We don't pity or look down on Protestants; we simply ask God to open their eyes to the fullness of Christ.

Alexios said his biggest lesson in life is patience—waiting and trusting God. This is not easy but will soften God's heart and He will give you strength to endure.

—*Monk (Alexios) of Xenophontos Monastery*

SADNESS

S aint Isaac the Syrian says sadness is not bad in itself; only sadness without hope is bad. Struggles are needed and are what create progress in the spiritual life. Depression is the result of love you have inside your spirit that is withheld from others. He stated that truly loving others is a cure for depression. If you make yourself right, then others will benefit.

Again, the monk reinforced the notion that comes from Isaac the Syrian: Any sadness as a result of sin or the passions that is not seen in the light of God's love and hope is from the evil one.

Sadness is not bad, but sadness without hope is a great sin and grieves our Lord.

—*Monk 1 from Iviron Monastery*

SUFFERING

People think that the spiritual life will make life easier by avoiding suffering, but rather it makes it possible to face the suffering with peace, joy, and dispassion. God accepts our passions but is repelled by constant complaints. Suffering and sadness are part of life, but we (the monks) don't focus on that. We keep calm and wait for God to act.

Bearing illnesses while glorifying God is higher than ascesis (spiritual struggle), because ascesis can be chosen and illness is not chosen. Ascesis is not a true sacrifice; rather it is like working on yourself. You do it for yourself, not others. Those who bear suffering and illness are dear to God, and His mercy is upon them.

The wounded bird still must fight for seeds and get nourishment, even though the healthy birds are winning. The wounded bird continues forward, getting what it needs and doing what it must. Also, animals are sad when their young are eaten or attacked. Even with this sadness, they do not stop moving forward and they continue to fly and have more chicks. We should be like the birds.

—*Monk 1 from Iviron Monastery*

Suffering and death are an entrance to eternal life.

—*Monk 2 from Iviron Monastery*

PRAYERS
FOR THE DEAD

During one of our discussions, we were encouraged to pray for the departed. The monk asked us to give him the names of those who had passed away. One of the young men in our group inquired why we would pray for someone whose life was over and there is no chance for them to repent.

The monk responded that God lives "outside of time," and has an eternal view of mankind. God intervenes in our life to help us with our salvation. He can see our whole life before Him, and he enters our life and gives us both blessings and crosses. He does this out of His extreme love for mankind, knowing that it is for the good and salvation of our souls. This eternal vision is unique to God (who is all knowing and all seeing) and allows Him to judge us in the light of eternity.

In a sense, God hears all our prayers—both past and present—and they are a factor in His salvific engagement with mankind. We live moment to moment (in time), but God with His mighty, loving, and eternal vision, can hear the prayers of his servants even before they are spoken. Therefore, we must continue to pray for the dead. God listens with an eternal ear, and our prayer for the dead becomes a reality in God's mind and can move Him to mercy and forgiveness.

Our love and our prayer for the departed transcend time and become a vehicle and plea for God's mercy. He said we must not confine God to our "constricted" world but realize that He is the eternal God who loves us and wants us to be saved. He chuckled and said, "God is looking for any excuse to save us, but we ignore Him and forget that He is a loving and forgiving Father." He said, "Never stop praying for our departed brothers and sisters."

—*Monk from Iviron Monastery*

JOY AND PEACE

The monks are no different from us. They struggle as well. Joy comes from a proper state of trying to do God's will. Some people who are sensitive can become sad. Peace is a fruit of prayer and Christian efforts. Faith cannot be acquired. It is earned as a gift if one can be diligent in the spiritual life and tries to find joy and peace in the presence of difficulties, fear, offenses, and suffering.

—*Monk 1 from Iviron Monastery*

STORIES TOLD
TO US

We were in the monastic office with the monks. Also present was a pious lawyer from Thessaloniki who is the lawyer for Iviron Monastery. As a young man, his father was condemned to death by the Nazis. His father had lived his life as an atheist, and he was a soccer fanatic. In prison the last night before his execution, a Greek guard came to his cell and gave him a New Testament. The guard said, "You are about to lose this life, don't lose the next life as well." He opened the book randomly, and read the verse that said, "Fear not, for I am with you." He spent the night reading the New Testament and was convinced that he would live. The guards came in the morning and said, "All executions are canceled; it is Hitler's birthday!" He was freed after six months. He went to the University of Thessaloniki, where he studied theology and became a humble professor, teaching at the junior high and high school levels. He did not want to return as a theologian to his home city, Xanthi, where he was known for his wild youth and soccer fanaticism. By God's providence, that is exactly where he ended up. He married and had five children—three boys and two girls. One of his sons is a well-known chanter. This pious lawyer chants with the Monks of Iviron and is respected by the whole monastic community as a brother. He told us that he and his father returned to Greece and found the now-elderly prison guard who gave him the New Testament. The lawyer made a three-hour recording of his father telling this story and has published it. It is distributed by the family free of charge.

Later, we were told a story about Aristotle Onassis. He was sailing the Mediterranean and stopped at Vatopedi Monastery. On the boat as guests were the elderly Winston Churchill and the famous opera star Maria Callas. Onassis told his wife that he and the men would go to the monastery, but women were not allowed on the Holy Mountain. When Onassis left, his wife was upset that she could not see Athos, so she told the captain to take her to shore so she could put her foot on the Holy Mountain. Defiantly, she placed her foot on the pier on Athos. When they reached the next port in Italy, Mrs. Onassis tripped when getting off the boat and broke the ankle of the same foot she put on the Holy Mountain. She had to be hospitalized and Onassis, without his wife, took his guests back to Scorpios Island. On this return voyage, Onassis developed a relationship with Maria Callas that eventually led to his divorce from his wife. Later in life, Mrs. Onassis wrote a letter to the government of Mount Athos, apologizing for violating the rule of no women on Athos. She claimed her life was never the same after that event. The letter still exists in the archives of Mount Athos.

✝✝✝

On the way to Elder Paisios's cell, we stopped at a hermit's hut. His name is Gabriel. He is an elderly monk living alone on the mountain. He invited us in and spoke to the group for thirty minutes. He spoke to us while lying down. He was disheveled, but joyous. He told jokes and gave us his wisdom. He said, "If you want to be a beggar, then store your things away. All we really own or keep is that which we give away. Burial garments are not made with any pockets!" His jokes were great. He wished for us family harmony and love and said, "Don't complain." He told of a woman who complained all the time about her husband. She told him, "If I had poison, I would give it to you!" He said, "Woman, if you had poison, I would take it!"

He also talked about possessions. He said a man bought a new car and took it to the priest for a blessing so he would not crash. Afterward, he had an accident, went back to the priest, and asked him, "Father, what kind of blessing did you give me because I crashed the car?" The priest asked, "How fast were you going?" He said, "Sixty miles per hour." The priest said, "Oh, that's the problem. The blessing is only good for fifty miles per hour!"

A man asked, "How can there be a God when we cannot see him?" He ridiculed the people who believed and said it's stupid and impossible to believe in something you cannot see. A wise priest said, "I see your shirt; does it exist?" "Of course," the man said. "I also see your boots; do they exist?" "Of course," the man said. "Well, I can't see your brain, so you must not have one to say such stupid things about God!"

The monks are humorous and light-hearted, full of joy and love. They enjoy a good joke. Father Gabriel blessed each of us and wished for Christ's blessing, harmony, and good jobs for the young men. He took our names for prayer. We asked for a final word for people in America, and he said, "Tell the people to give to the poor."

In the morning service, this beautiful monk came to us and said goodbye. He said it was nice to have us. He is a kind and gentle man.

EPILOGUE

My hope is that the reader has absorbed some of the wisdom that was imparted to me during my journeys to Mount Athos over the past fourteen years. The lessons I received were not only from the words spoken to me, but also from the example of holy men living a life dedicated to prayer, work, and worship. I have learned that love and humility are the guiding lights of human existence. We must especially love our enemies. This is the measure of a true Christian. The saints of the Church exhibited this love, even for those who tortured and killed them. Christ was filled with these attributes, and I pray that we all can acquire some measure of both. As my dear Γιαγιά (grandmother) would say in all circumstances: "Ο Θεός είναι μεγάλος! (God is Great!)"

ABOUT THE MONKS

Monk 1 from Iviron Monastery

This young monk was a favorite of mine. He has spent much of his adult life on the Holy Mountain. His father had left his mother, and he was raised by an American G.I. who married his mother and became a positive role model for him. He lived in America for a short time, but returned to Greece at a young age. He found a home at Iviron Monastery and is a *schema* (highest order) monk.

Monk from Vatopedi Monastery

He was a graduate of Stanford University and studied engineering. He said he is still an engineer. An engineer's job and, his job now as a monk, is to find and solve problems. He is an engineer of the soul. He laughed.

Monk 2 from Iviron Monastery

He was born in Japan. He became Protestant and developed his monastic roots there. Silence and dispassion are of particular importance in his life.

Monk 3 from Iviron Monastery

He was born in Australia and has spent most of his adult life on Mount Athos. He is also a priest and exhibits a particularly quiet and peaceful demeanor. He was always willing to discuss spiritual matters with us pilgrims. Australia has one million Orthodox, which is 5 percent of the population. His brother is a priest in Australia. Communion on Holy Saturday can take three hours in the church in Australia.

Saint Porphyrios of Mount Athos

Monk (Alexios) of Xenophontos

Alexios is the abbot of Xenophontos. He met with us in his private quarters. It was truly a blessing. He is a truly holy Athonite spiritual father. He sees the mission of the monastery to receive and give rest and refreshment to visitors and pilgrims.

Monk 2 from Xenophontos Monastery

He is a woodworker who has been on the Holy Mountain for forty years!

Monk 3 from Xenophontos Monastery

He was a convert who was at Holy Cross seminary in Boston. He was never sure he wanted to be a priest, and considered becoming a professor. He visited Mount Athos for one to two months on his own, and decided to follow monasticism at Xenophontos.

He has been there for seventeen years. He comes from an evangelical background. His mother died two years previously from Alzheimer's, and his father died eleven years before we saw him. He never saw them again after he left Boston. His mother never wanted him to know she was ill so he wouldn't be pulled back home. He seemed sad when he spoke of this. He is a friend and seminary classmate of Father George Dokos, our former priest at St. Mary's Greek Orthodox Church in Minneapolis, Minnesota.

ACKNOWLEDGEMENTS

I would especially like to thank and acknowledge Becky Myerly and Sophia Patane for their encouragement and tireless editing of this manuscript. It was a blessing to have their help along this journey. Dr. Harry Boosalis was our loving and faithful guide and teacher on these pilgrimages. I thank him from the bottom of my heart. I am especially thankful for my children, Michael, Emily, and Gabriel, and my son-in-law Perry, for the love and respect they have shown me over the years. They are and always will be my pride and joy.

ABOUT
THE AUTHOR

Steven Michael Rakes is a lifelong member of the Greek Orthodox Church. He grew up in the Midwest (Omaha, Nebraska) and has made his home in Minneapolis, where he lives with Popie, his wife of 41 years. He has three adult children and three grandchildren. He is a practicing physician and surgeon. In his spare time, he enjoys reading the Fathers of the Church and volunteering whenever possible at his home parish, St. Mary's Greek Orthodox Church in Minneapolis. The highlight of his spiritual life has been his trips to Mt. Athos. He is hopeful that this collection will be an inspiration to all who read it.